Ladders

Living in the DESERT

Communities We Live In

Prickly Plants

by Nathan W. James

There are places in the world where it hardly ever rains and water is scarce. They are called **deserts**. A desert only gets a small amount of rain each year. Most deserts are quite hot. Even so, many living things make their home there. One type of plant flourishes in a desert—the **cactus**.

This is the Sonoran Desert in Arizona. Many different types of cacti grow in this desert. Some have thick, straight trunks. Others are shaped like a barrel. Some have flat, leaflike pads. These pads can look like the wide end of a boat paddle.

If you've ever touched a cactus, you'll know it's not like other plants. It has a waxy coating that helps it hold water inside. In fact, cacti (more than one cactus) are made up mostly of water. Many cacti have sharp needles poking out from their stems instead of leaves. Needles protect a cactus from animals that might try to harm it. Most animals don't want to be poked by the pointy needles. Some clever creatures have learned to avoid them to get what they want—the water inside the cactus.

Thirsty desert animals sometimes scratch their way into a cactus to eat its watery insides. These animals carefully avoid the protective needles. Then they dig through the waxy coating. On a blazing hot desert day, they will work long and hard to enjoy a cool piece of cactus.

A Gila woodpecker hollows out a hole in a saguaro cactus. Inside, it makes its nest. Screech owls and other animals might move in after the woodpecker leaves.

As Tall As a House

Cacti provide desert animals with more than just food and water. There are hardly any trees in deserts. Birds must find other places to build nests. Some birds, such as the Gila (HEE-luh) woodpecker, peck holes in cacti to make cozy homes. A hole in a cactus is a perfect place for a woodpecker to nest.

Other birds choose to live in saguaro (suh-WAH-ro) cacti. The saguaro is what most people think of when they think of a cactus. You've probably seen them in a cartoon. Saguaros only grow in the Sonoran Desert. That's a desert that stretches from the western United States to Mexico. The saguaro is the tallest cactus in the United States. It can grow taller than a one-story house. It has bent "arms" that grow from a tall center stem.

A saguaro cactus usually begins to sprout a branch out of its side when it's 50 to 70 years old. That may sound old to you, but it's young for a saguaro. These tall cacti can live to be 200 years old!

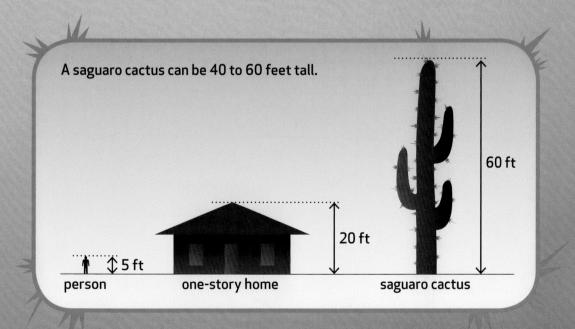

A saguaro cactus can be 40 to 60 feet tall.

5 ft — person

20 ft — one-story home

60 ft — saguaro cactus

Cactus for Lunch

The saguaro only lives in the Sonoran Desert, but the prickly pear cactus grows in hot deserts all over the world. Prickly pears are shorter than saguaro cacti. They only grow to be seven feet tall, or a little taller than a grown man. The prickly pear cactus is another desert plant that makes a good home for small animals and birds. The thick pads and needles of this cactus protect birds from enemies that might attack their nests.

Prickly pear cacti make good lunches for humans—minus the needles, of course. People cook and then eat prickly pear pads

Farmers pick nopales and bring them to markets.

called *nopales* (no-PAH-layz). First, the cactus needles are boiled or plucked off the flat, leafy pads. Then the pads are grilled and served like a steak. They taste a little like green beans.

Prickly pear cacti get their name from their fruit. The fruit looks like a pear with small spines. When the prickly pear fruit is ripe, it is bright red. It can be cut in half and eaten like a cantaloupe. Many people use the pears to make jams and jellies. They taste a little like watermelon bubble gum, and they turn your tongue just as red.

> Nopales salad

This woman is cleaning nopales pads at a market. She wears gloves to make sure she isn't pricked by the nopales' needles. The needles are small and hard to see.

Check In Why do cacti have a waxy coating and needles instead of leaves?

SANDY SETTLE

by Jennifer A. Smith

Hairy, Scary

A desert is a tough place to live. It can be very hot during the day and very cold when the sun goes down. It gets little rain. But many animals make the desert their home in spite of these harsh conditions. Let's look at how these animals have **adapted** to living in the desert—how their bodies are designed to live and survive in this hot, dry place.

The tarantula (tuh-RAN-chuh-luh) is a very large, hairy spider. It lives in the deserts of the United States and Mexico. During the day, the tarantula sleeps in a **burrow**. That's a hole that is dug in the sand. Daytime is much hotter than nighttime in the desert. The tarantula avoids the heat by sleeping during the day. And because its burrow is underground, it stays cooler than the ground above.

The tarantula comes out to hunt for its food at night, when temperatures drop. Like other spiders, the tarantula mainly eats insects. It does not spin a web, though. It catches its food by pouncing on it. Fortunately, the desert is full of bugs to snack on!

< Tarantulas know when other animals are near. They feel tiny motions through the ground and in the air.

9

The Horse of the Desert

Camels have been helping humans travel and transport heavy loads through deserts for thousands of years. Most camels have one hump, but some camels have two. They are called Bactrian (BAK-tree-uhn) camels, and they live in rocky deserts in Asia. These deserts are very hot in summer and very cold in winter.

Many people think camels use their humps for storing water. Actually, camels store fat in their humps. Their bodies can use that fat for energy when food is hard to find.

∨ These Bactrian camels are crossing a desert in China.

Camels have adapted to survive for a long time without food and water. This allows these animals to live in **arid**, or dry, climates. Bactrian camels can even survive on just the water they get from eating the grasses that grow in the desert during the winter.

Like one-humped camels, Bactrian camels have nostrils that can shut tight to keep blowing desert sand out of their noses. Bactrian camels grow a special thick coat of hair to keep them warm in the cold desert winters. They shed their coats quickly when summer comes. That's so they don't get too hot in the desert sun.

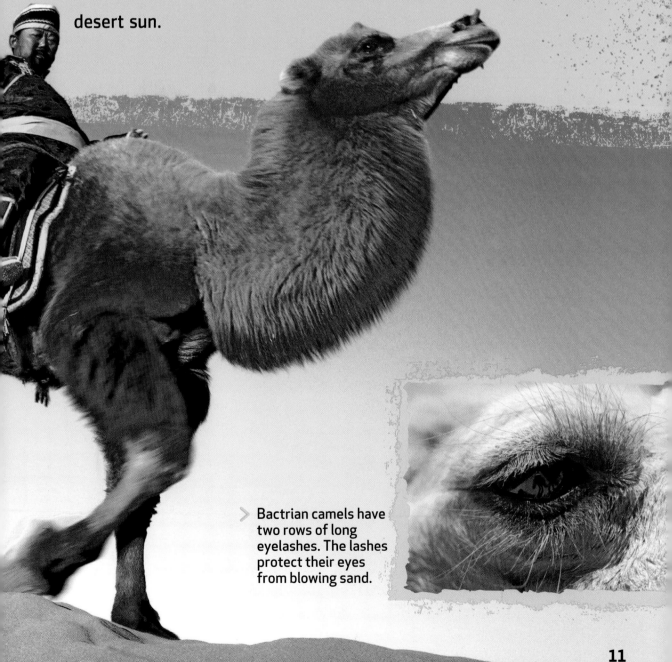

> Bactrian camels have two rows of long eyelashes. The lashes protect their eyes from blowing sand.

Made for Desert Living

The kangaroo rat is a **rodent** that lives in the arid deserts of the United States, Canada, and Mexico. A rodent is a small animal with big front teeth for chewing. Mice and squirrels are rodents. The kangaroo rat has adapted to desert living. It has large back feet that help it hop and jump quickly through desert sand.

The kangaroo rat has one behavior that really helps it live in the desert. It almost never drinks water! It gets all the water it needs from eating the seeds of desert plants.

This kangaroo rat peeks from its burrow.

Like the tarantula, the kangaroo rat digs a burrow in the ground. The burrow protects the kangaroo rat from the heat of the desert. The kangaroo rat only leaves its burrow at night to search for seeds. It gathers them in the pouches in its cheeks and brings them back to the burrow where it stores them. If the desert sun gets too hot, or if a rare rainstorm comes, the kangaroo rat will have enough stored food to stay in its burrow for days.

Though kangaroo rats have many predators, or animals that hunt them for food, they have excellent hearing to help them stay safe. They listen carefully for approaching animals—even owls flying quietly overhead. Then they can escape into their burrows before it's too late.

❮ Kangaroo rats don't sweat. That means their bodies keep a lot of water.

A Desert Monster

The Gila (HEE-luh) monster isn't a monster at all. It's a big lizard found in the deserts of the United States and Mexico. It can grow to be nearly two feet long, and it can weigh up to five pounds.

The Gila monster gets water from the food it eats. It raids the nests of desert birds to eat their eggs. It also eats small animals. Like a camel stores fat in its humps, the Gila monster stores fat in its tail. This allows it to go many months in between meals, living off its stored fat.

The Gila monster lives in a burrow just like the tarantula and kangaroo rat. It spends nearly all of its time there, away from the desert heat. In fact, it only comes out of the entrance once in a while to hunt or to warm itself in the sun.

Though Gila monsters do have a poisonous bite, they only use it to protect themselves from threatening enemies. They really aren't dangerous to people.

A Gila monster's skin has orange, yellow, or pink patterns. The colors tell animals that the Gila monster is poisonous.

Check In Tell how one of the animals you read about has adapted to living in the desert.

Desert Pen Pals

by Nathan W. James

There are deserts all over the world. Some are hot, some are cold, but all of them are dry. Meet two students who live in desert communities. Let's follow them as they email back and forth about where they live.

Hi Aya,

Hello from the city of Tucson (TOO-sahn), Arizona! My name is Elena, and I am 9 years old. Arizona is a state in the United States that has deserts. I learned from my teacher that Siwa Oasis is also in a desert, but in the country of Egypt. Could you please tell me about where you live? I'm glad our teachers arranged for us to email each other! Here's a picture of me with my dog and a picture of my house.

'Bye! Elena 😊

Hi Elena,

I am also 9, and I'm happy to email you! What is your cute dog's name?

I've attached pictures of me and my little brother, Omar, and of Siwa Oasis. An **oasis** is a surprising place because it has lots of plants and water, even though it is in the middle of a desert. Siwa Oasis is in the Sahara, a desert that covers most of my country, Egypt.

It's hot here most of the year, and we get very little rain, but it gets as cold as 48°F in winter. When it's that cold, Omar and I don't like to play outside.

Email me back! Aya

Hey Aya!

My dog's name is Thunder. We got him during a thunderstorm, so it's a good name. It rains and storms a lot here during the monsoon season. A **monsoon** is a windy, heavy rainstorm, and here in Tucson, the monsoon season starts in June and can last until September. Sometimes it feels like I'm wearing my rain boots all summer. It's pretty hot and dry the rest of the year. You can see from the picture I'm sending that you and Omar wouldn't like to play outside during the monsoon season either! ☹

Talk to you soon! Elena

Hi Elena,

The picture you sent of the monsoon is frightening. It does not thunderstorm often in Siwa Oasis. In fact, it almost never rains here. But, on windy days, sand blows into our faces from all of the sand dunes in the desert near us. Sand dunes are mountains of sand that shift in the wind.

Sometimes we have to cover our mouths with our clothes so we don't breathe in the blowing sand. You and Thunder would not like windy days here.

Hope to hear back from you soon! Aya

Hello Aya,

What kinds of food do you eat in Egypt? Do you have a favorite food? Tacos are my favorite meal. They are tortillas (tor-TEE-yuhs)—a kind of flat bread—filled with spicy meat. Every Saturday night, my family gets tacos from my favorite restaurant (see my picture), and I always give Thunder a little. Tacos are his favorite food, too!

You wrote that your town doesn't get much rain, so where does the water you drink come from? Most of our water comes from a big river many miles away. We try not to use too much extra water here. 😋

Later! Elena

TAQUERIA

TAQUERIA

·TACOS
·TORTAS
·BURROS
·MARISCOS
·SEA FOOD

·HORCHATA
·LIMONADA
·FOUNTAIN DRINKS

Dear Elena, 😃

We get our water from **springs**, or fresh water flowing from deep in the ground. Springs are all over Siwa Oasis, and the spring water makes our oasis beautiful by helping trees and plants grow.

The tacos in your picture look delicious. I wish Siwa Oasis had a taco restaurant so I could try them. We eat many kinds of foods in Egypt, but my favorite is falafel, made of ground chickpeas patted into balls and fried. My mother makes bread to wrap the falafel in, and it looks a little like tacos. I wish I could email you some to taste!

Here's my father sitting behind a falafel dinner. I helped mom make the dinner to celebrate Omar's football team's success. You call football "soccer" in the United States, right? Do you play a sport?

Email again soon! Aya

Hi Aya, 😊

I am sending you and Omar a picture of my softball team. I'm standing at home plate dressed in a gray and black uniform. I'm a good batter. I've hit three home runs this year so far. Last year my team won almost all of our games!

I like to take short bike rides to warm up before a game. Today, I saw three lizards while I rode my bike. A lot of lizards live in the desert, and I have decided that seeing lizards before a game is a sign that my team will win.

This message makes me wonder if you play a sport, Aya.

Email me back! Elena

Dear Elena,

I don't play sports, even though Omar tries to get me to play football with him and his friends from the neighborhood. They play right across the street from our house, so I sometimes walk over there to cheer my brother on. Here is a picture I have taken of one of their games. Maybe one day I will join them and play!

We have lizards here in Siwa Oasis, too, and I like watching them climb on the walls. Sometimes I try to catch one when it is sunning itself, but it always runs away!

I enjoy our emails! Aya

Check In Describe how Aya and Elena's lives are similar and different in their desert communities.

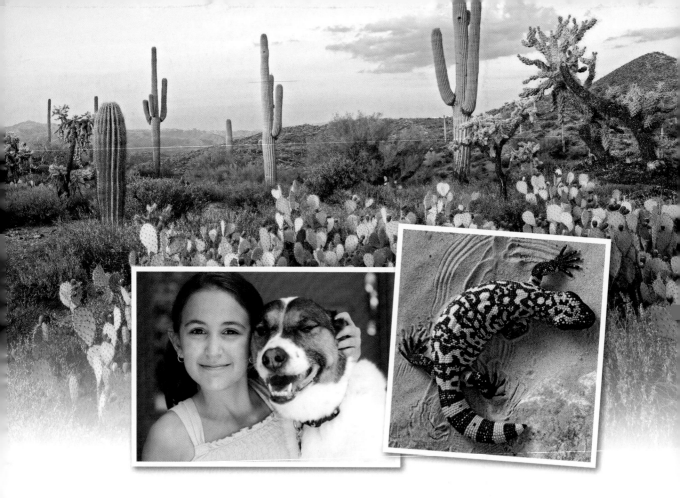

Discuss

1. What do you think connects the three selections you read in this book? What makes you think that?

2. How do saguaro and prickly pear cacti provide homes and food to living things in the desert?

3. Describe how some plants and animals are adapted to live in land as dry as the desert.

4. Would you like to live in a desert community like the ones you read about? Why or why not?

5. What do you still want to know about deserts and desert communities? How can you learn more?